One
Heart
Opening

Other Books by Ellen Grace O'Brian

The Sanctuary of Belonging

Living the Eternal Way
Spiritual Meaning and Practice for Daily Life

One
Heart
Opening

■

Poems
for the
Journey
of
Awakening

Center for Spiritual Enlightenment

One Heart Opening
Poems for the Journey of Awakening

Cover and book design by Anne Adden, Adden Design

ISBN 0-9660518-2-3

Center for Spiritual Enlightenment
Post Office Box 112185
Campbell, California 95011-2185
Telephone: (408) 244-5151
email: cse@best.com

*For
Jill
and
Forrest*

Contents

I
Signs

The Night Before the Wedding

At the door to the wedding chamber
he said, "I will have what I want
and you will say yes to me.
What I want will be what you want too;
I have always said yes to you."

She recoiled in ancient fear
saying, "No, you cannot have me in this way.
Where is my groom who will dance
the heart's rhythm with me
across this threshold?"

For an instant, under
the white lace of her femininity,
he saw the knife —
the one that would kill him,
open him, and expose the marrow
he kept covered.
Men always want to keep a little something hidden,
something they do not open, or share.
Women want it all.

In that same instant,
she saw, under his black coat,
the dark pool where she would drown —
her cries unheard in the night
as she went down alone.
Women always want a point of reference,
a way to see the relationship between this and that.
Men want to move ahead and say, "Let it go."

Men are stupid.
They walk over what they have
without recognizing it, breaking
the delicate ties that support them as they go.

Women are insane.
They have everything
and do not know it.
They always want more and
lose a little each time they bargain.

The night before the wedding
she dreams of his mother
coming into their house
and cleaning their kitchen.
The mother complains she has eaten too much
her intestines are grumbling and
she cannot digest it all.

The groom eats and grows fat
the bride fasts and weeps
The ancient beasts have begun their rites
and no one sleeps through the night.

The one who will give the blessing
lights a candle and prays.

Josephine and Her Daughter

Divine Mother is an old Italian woman
smoking cigarettes on the porch
with her daughter. She keeps
her beauty under her hat,
while her feet and hands imitate
winter sycamore trees
cut back from their fullness
without mercy.

In spring the fullness
shows itself again
a wild green canopy

children sit underneath
and tell her story.
The one of love
of the old country
of sacrifice and the silence

that goes on speaking
through the generations
like the waves
washing the boat
on its way
to America.

■ *Signs of the Neighborhood*

"And the Lord showed signs and wonders. . ."
Deuteronomy 6:22

"And there shall be signs in the sun, and in the moon, and in the stars; and upon the earth distress of nations, with perplexity; the sea and the waves roaring. . ."
Luke 21:25

Aviso!
Agua contaminado. The small creek
that runs through our neighborhood
this morning has a sign: Beware!
The tree holds the sign
stands next to the creek
roots touch creek bed wetness
leaves reflect back water light
a silent witness

the family member grown mute
in an instant of unspeakable horror.
The one who does not speak a word again
but remains in that place where
the whole scene remains with her
and replays when you look in her eyes.
Of the thousand details
not one is lost.
Look closely
the tiny veins connect:
a pattern familiar
to the course of history.

The water, moving over rocks,
is not silent. It still sings.
She Who Grasps Us,
holds us in her beauty, invites
us in to remember
water joy, floating in the mother
feeding on her earth body
breathing with the heartbeat
this morning says: What have you done?

■ *Walking with My Father*

Joining you and the dog
on your morning walk through the hills
I take note: at seventy five
you are still stronger than me.
Out of breath, I try to keep pace

with your determination.
The dog stops and starts
provides us with conversation
finally after seventy years
the boy gets a dog

but you are disappointed in her too.
She loves my mother more than you,
prefers her lap to yours, comes to you
only for food. Cupboard love! you declare it.
In the distance I see the old house
witness to the angry wound

ungrateful children who come infrequently,
refuse to pay homage, instead cry out to you:
It was not enough!
We are not as sinister as Lear's daughters
nor you, our king, as foolish but we are equally afraid

you of the unforgiving dust your parents left behind,
us of the plenty that grew from your buried grief.
Everything that ground gave up to us was ransomed.
Like generations before us
we paid with our childhood.
The ghost of Cordelia walks with you now
and says, nothing.

■ *Witchgrass*

I sit on the back steps joining
meter boxes and garbage cans
and I watch you
skip along
the asphalt
a broken stick against
the cyclone fence
your small legs brushed by
summer's first weeds.
How like them you are
as you court the wind
with ladies curtsies,
if you please,
capturing the sun's rays with
stray yellow hair.
They grow with the sun
in spite of the asphalt,
through the cyclone fence.
And you,
I see you grow too
in spite of me
you break through, as if
I were mother of softest earth.
You bring me bouquets
of back alley weeds
and I cry.

■ *Love Poems*

I have been looking for my words
that I stored like bottled water
just in case.
I would spell it out now, and say
I love you
but you have taken them.
At night, I find them
hovering in the shadows of your body.
They gape at me like goldfish.

■ *Clothes*

Cleaning the house is easier
than listening to my mind.
It's a woman's body work, where
the mind beast is temporarily soothed
by folding the sheets and stacking the shirts,
their sleeves pressed against the back.
Into the folds I breathe

what I cannot say to you.
I learned this from my mother;
the clothes we wore carried her.
Sometimes they were lost, her chaos
revealing itself in a pile of rumpled laundry
waiting to be sorted and pressed.

The pile would grow with my father's anger
at what could not be controlled.
He built her a laundry bin in the garage
to hide the clothes, so large
I climbed into it and hid.

The clothes remained tangled in their silent dance
until we outgrew them and gave them away.
I wonder about the girl
wearing the magenta and gold plaid dress,
the one I wore on the first day of school,
laid out so carefully on the bed the night before
to step into that morning like a new life.
I wonder can she tell the dress is full of dreams,
my mother's and mine.

■ *Going Away*

I watch the girl down the street
the one who is reed thin
the one whose eyes dart
whose eyes say: I
do not live here
do not try to see

me, I have gone
gone with the nights
gone with my mother
in jail with her thoughts
how to get out and
get her next fix.

When she comes to our door,
one child among many who
sell tickets for school,
I buy from her.
I want to say

you can do this
you can live
you can hold your head up
but she is gone
does not look at me
does not say,
thanks.

In my dream
she comes to the door
much younger, brown
full body, and soft eyes.
I invite her in,
embrace her, say
I am so glad you are here.

In my dream
she lets me hold her, feel
her small warm breath,
her sweet hair damp
at the edges of her scalp.
I drift back on the scent
of her skin to another time,
and another girl going away.

■ *Autumn*

All you have tried to hold on to
is leaving you now, even your
prayers will not save you from this.
They will only speed the loss.
Brightness grows dark
in a closed container.

All around you are
autumn woods, where
leaves bright rainfall
take the breath
into the blessed body
of silence.

In the temple
the rabbi and the cantor
consort against eternity,
filling the service with the sound
of their own voices calling.
Page numbers in the prayerbook
become a Hebrew do-si-do,
allemande left. Breathless
the congregation stands,
mostly in pairs, and shuffles
through the pages of time—
here the mourners,
there the celebrants.

No use blaming the rabbi,
without his leadership
the congregation falls
into the prayers of the common tongue:
how are the children
were they home for the holidays
her husband had a stroke last month
look how things change.

Each leaf falling
speaks a prayer, filling
the forest with silence
the color of grace.
Each one dropped into
its own fullness of time
while eternity
spins toward earth.

The eyes of the sage
grow brighter with time.
The body has been opened —
me and my and need have escaped,
a small voice unheeded
in the roar of silence.

While it is autumn
there is still time for you.
Go into your solitary house
where the drawers of memory
gape in musty betrayal,
too full to close.
Open all the doors and windows,
hear the cry of each leaf falling:
I am alone!
Breathe the air of that silence
into your fast fading bones
find where your marrow beat
sings the same symphony
then you will know
how vast is this aloneness,
how full.

II
Healings

■ *Desert Moon*

desert moon rising
illuminating
earth constellations
wildflowers on sand
born again
so fragile
against the wind

For Ann, at 56

Women who climb mountains
must follow the heart's terrain.
You are no different with
your nights on the desert,
plotting out star maps
for your next journey.
You have opened the circle wide

tossed the stones named for
children, lovers, friends —
even your parents are dust now

their voices echo like a rattler's tail shed,
impotent in the wind, a skeleton
of your former days.
They have lost their bite.
You have gathered your medicine,
know the antidotes, watch where you step.
Now it is time to sing.

Gather the bones of your next life,
fill them with the marrow
of your true voice.
The words you will need are written
on the wings of the angel who stands
there, over your childhood dream
there, over the one you left behind.

Burying the Gold
A Story for My Husband

The small girl,
awakened by her drunken father
that night, learned this:
She could not win.

He was disturbed,
disturbed past anger.
Coming home walking through
the kitchen
there was a feeling
he did not like, or
perhaps it was a sound.
Someone spilled juice on the floor
and didn't clean it up right.
It left a residue.
A sticky residue of something.
Something that stopped him
when he came in
in the middle of the night.
Maybe that sticky feeling
said something to him,
maybe he heard right out loud,
"Things are out of control here!" or,
"No one cares!"
Who knows.
The walls actually said those things
all of the time there
but he played loud music
when he got home at night
so he didn't hear them.
Maybe that sticky residue

just made it impossible for him to imagine
on such a night that he slipped silently
past them all, sleeping.

She had long ago learned
to sleep with one eye open,
scanning the horizon
for his return.

He said he wanted the truth.
The truth would be all that mattered.
Did she do it?
If she said no,
he would keep her up all night interrogating her,
If she said yes,
he would beat her.

She said no. Then,
when she got too tired,
she said yes.
She spoke that yes
with the only power she could find.
Like a silent star falling in the sky
she said inside, I will not feel.
And she didn't.
The sting of his hand on
her bare flesh was dull, and
there was no sound.
No sound and no feeling.
Just a falling sensation,
falling inside, in slow motion.

When it was over
she walked to her room
and there were no tears.
There was only that slight tremor
at her chin, the falling away inside and
her own knowing: she had become his daughter.

The next morning she set out
on her own
taking what she cared most about
and feared to leave behind
A small doll carriage
packed with two baby dolls and their clothes.
She would not leave them there.
She took her souvenir from the fieldtrip
to the lost goldmine,
a small vial filled with water and tiny flecks of gold.
She knew the gold was valuable
and it wasn't safe in that house.
What she didn't know was:
it was already lost.

She walked, pushing the carriage,
the dolls and their clothes,
and the vial.
She walked past all of the houses on the street.
She walked past the school,
past the corner store where she sometimes
took her pennies to buy sweets
to change a bitter day.
She walked to the orchards

at the edge of what she knew
She didn't discuss the predicament with the dolls,
so as not to worry them.
She pretended that she didn't already know what she would do.
She pretended that she had options.

Before she went back
she dug a hole in the orchard
and buried the gold.
She planned to return for it when it was time.
She didn't really think about the gold again
until the day she saw the tractors
digging up the earth in the old orchard
making foundations for the new homes.
The dolls had long since passed on
losing hair and limbs along the way to
the forgetting of their names.
The trees now down
the orchard turned over and she
so much older, feared:
something was lost that cannot be recovered.
There was no real pain in this.
The pain was that of a phantom limb
long ago cut away,
sending signals
out into empty space.

And so I tell you this story for her
because I think you should know
when you give her the gold necklace

on her birthday
the bracelet as a valentine
the ring at the wedding

The small girl,
still sleeping with one eye open,
looks to see:
Has it returned?

■ *Sometimes at Night*

Sometimes at night
a light shines, here,
in the middle of my chest
and I see you
innocence is your face
everything you have ever done
washes up
on this shore of love.
You walk through it all
breathe in the salt air
step across the tangled kelp
enter another life.

Early Morning

You speak softly, and the wild geese
eat from your hand.

This early morning
mixed with mild green
you wait on the lake's edge
while she approaches with
ancient songs of power,
lest you doubt her.

Her young spin small circles
and wait.

The exchange is made too quickly
witnessed only by your hand
now empty.

Her scolding song delights you
into imagining you have given freely.
Then the gift returns,
a reflection on rippled water
and the sound of wings.

■ *Lazarus Girl*

I called you Lazarus girl
when after four days and nights
you walked out of death's tomb.
I could see your face shining

through the grave clothes.
It was then, I wept.
Every mother tells herself:
If only I had been there,
this would not have happened.
And so at your bedside I prayed:

Please God, let me be here now.
When the nurse invited me to
bathe you before the surgery,
I knew I was given

a second chance. And I took it.
There was not one part of you
I left unblessed, unnoticed, or

unloved. I bathed you
holy, as if for the first
and the last time;
and I was satisfied
in that moment

of loving you
that if love itself
had the power to roll the stone away
and shout: Come forth!
my hands that touched your body
with the heart's full attention
had surely spoken the word.

■ *Surrender*

The ocean does not
argue with the rock.
It goes where it will,
telling the secret, again
then again, to the slow
moving cliffs. Mossy
fingers grope in prayer
facing the horizon at dawn.

Listen for the secret.
Ah! When it is heard
one more
jagged edge
lets go.

Poem for the New Year

I, a woman with pale skin
who burns easily, this year
dream of being a native woman with
dark skin who comes into this life
prepared to soak up
its light and beauty

with nakedness and ease.
Already this year there is
so much light;
I am planning how
to take it in.

Sunscreens no longer protect me
as the days get longer and brighter
I consider: It really isn't that hole
in the ozone, manmade.
It's the one in my heart.
Although it too started way back then
when aerosol first came in and
everything in the house was so clean,
it was sterilized. You could eat
off the floor, its linoleum cracks
scrubbed with a toothbrush.
My mother,on her hands and knees,
protected us all from germs
except that one, the one
we never talked about,
the one that ate
into the hearts of all of us
made us cover ourselves and go

fearing both the darkness and the light,
unable to find that place
where kindness lives.
The simplest things were lost
back then: a loving glance, sweet words,
acts of generosity, hand on a hand, a warm touch.

This year they have all
come back
like the wildflower
in the woods
that appears only in certain years
when conditions are right.

The promises of this year
blind me. And so I begin it
blind but sensitive to its
atmosphere, like a baby
breathing for the first time.
The breath is a joyous pain
signaling the separation
we cannot live without and
the union we go seeking.

I have deemed myself, and you,
possible this year. Those little holes
in the heart, we will use them.
We will use them to breathe through
becoming new creatures with gills
swimming in the light world,
at last at home in the deep.

▪ *Standing in Her Place*

That morning when I turned
back toward our bed,
the light was on your face
and I saw him.
He was three, or four,
his arms stretched out —
eyes, hands, mouth, legs, feet,

open, his whole body smiling.
Then, I saw her, too.
She was there, too,
standing by the side of the bed
arms folded across her chest
deciding once again
whether to withhold or to give
tell him yes, or no.
It must have been no.

Then he says, "I didn't do anything wrong."
He says, "I was just being
happy." When I hear this
I cannot breathe
I hold very still, I'm afraid
I am standing in her place.
I know he has returned

to hear the yes.
It is a sacred trust,
I do not turn away.

III
Invocations

■ *Enlightenment*

We awaken to the Divine Presence
within us and around us and continue
to do our duty in this lifetime.

Viewed from the outside
it looks just the same.
But inside —
the soul is singing —
Oh the wood!
Oh the water!

■ *The Woman Whose Heart Belongs to God* *(from Proverbs 31)*

Who can find a strong woman?
She cannot be bought or seduced;
she is worthy beyond diamonds.
She opens the heart of her husband to trust,
and stops the war in him.
She walks in the direction of light
all the days of her life.
She seeks harmony with nature; the work of her heart
and her hands willingly follow the way.
She overflows with creativity
like the merchants' ships bringing food from afar.
Her light shines in the darkness,
and nourishes everyone around her.
She discerns where to invest her time and her energy:
the seedlings of her handwork become a vineyard.
She treats her body as a sacred temple,
strong pillars are her arms and her legs.
She knows who she is; her awareness burns
like a candle through the night.
She transforms her talents into meaningful work.
She stretches out her hands to the poor, yes,
with compassion she reaches for those in need.
She is not afraid of death for her household,
for all her household are clothed with the Mother's scarlet.
She makes her life rich, a tapestry of silk and purple.
Her husband is a righteous man,
respected in the community among the elders.
She knows the value of her work in the world,
and contributes to the weave of life.
Strength and honor are her clothing,

and joy follows her into the future.
She speaks with wisdom and
kindness flows from her tongue.
She eats the bread of life,
and brings awareness to her household.
Her children flourish, and call her blessed;
her husband praises her too.
Her father and mother know
she is the shining one.
She is not deceived by flattery, or affected by her beauty:
True praise belongs to the woman
whose heart belongs to God.
She is given the fruit of her hands,
and her own works praise her in the gates.

■ *A Devotee's Prayer*

This life of God's
I surrender to God
and hold nothing back.

This moment of God's
I give to God
and let go of expectation.

This heart of God's
I give to God
may it's song
be the song of forgiveness.

These hands of God's
I give to God
may their work
be the work of healing.

■ *Everything that Happens to Me Now*

Retreating into the heart
I am joyously alone with you
I am the empty cup overflowing
I am dark eyes opening to the light
I am the dawn waking to this day.
Everything that happens to me now
speaks your name.

■ *Heather*

You, a budding pink evergreen,
hearty enough to withstand
the changes of climate
that came with your childhood.
Constant uprooting taught you:
you can grow in more than one place.
You came into this life
determined to bloom.

Rare girl
cradled in your father's arms,
raised on grandfather wisdom,
stepping inside the circle
of your seventeenth year
you learn of your grandmothers,
the wisdom Rachel hid under their skirts.
You meet your true mother
as if for the first time.
After this, you will meet her again and again
in the women who bless you,
in those who curse you, too.
You will meet her in your own body

Your body will be the Torah of your Mother.
This is where you will learn to trust.
Imagine! All the sacred pilgrimage sites
are in your woman's body.

The prayer shawl now on your head
is not a cover to separate you
from that which is divine.
The silk that frames your hair
is the raising of the huppah in the desert;
inside you will find sweet honey and bread.

Your life will become your own as you declare it,
as you live the responsibility of your words.
It is your voice, not your words, but your voice
that will liberate you. When your parents hear it
they will let you go, with the same
joyous pain they felt at your birth.

■ *At San Juan Bautista*

I remember
being with you
at San Juan Bautista —
the troops had stopped marshalling,
readying for the next assault, and
planning my defense.
In that moment —
they were not to be found,
simply disappeared
into nothingness, where
I was alone with you,
so apparent.

I look for you now
in these times of war
in the city, where bombs
fall all through the night.
I cannot sleep
for missing you.

Krishna Sings the Mother Song
So Her Daughters Can Hear

Mary Mother of God, Kali, Durga,
Avalokiteshvara, Kwan Yin,
Shekinah, Krishna, Sophia,
O Divine Mother
of many names and forms
who is her self never changing,
I call to you now with my prayer.
The prayer of my eyes that see you
in cosmic dreams and blue earth turning,
in fields of light remembrance far off.
Beneath my feet on the dark forest floor
tiny stars of night lily white and blue
whisper forget me not, while I promise:
I will not. With each step I pray
I will not, knowing with the next breath
I will. Mother who stands still
while all else turns and changes, I pray:
Change me too. Change everything in me
that is not you. Mother Divine I have been
drifting in my little boat in your lapis sea,
rocking in your compassionate arms;
wake me now from my slumber of delusion
and my dreams of you. Let me embrace you
now in the light of your day and the darkness
of your night, make my body your home and
my heart your pillow. Ah! To recline with you
hold to your wisdom as a granddaughter tarries

with her grandmother, seeking her own wise future
in the eyes of love. You are the true mother,
wise companion, compassionate friend,
grandmother, guru, lover, husband, and child.
Nowhere can I turn that you are not:
You are the inspiration,
You are the seed and the blossom
of new life. O Mother Krishna,
your blue body shining,
when I close my eyes to all distraction
then I am alone with you. Too brief is our time!
I cry like a child reaching for her Mother's skirt:
Stay with me Mother, stay with me now.
Teach me to sing your song of life.
All of your daughters are weeping;
teach us your song.
Sing it to us Mother,
sing it to us now.

■ *Muse*

When she visits me
(it is not often, now)
I make a simple offering,
rice from my kitchen
steaming in a small white bowl.
She seasons it, pouring delicately
the dark, salty, sauce.
We do not talk, but listen
(to some quieter things)
like the movement of clouds,
those phantom freight trains
that connect, and ride low
across the evening sky.

■ *Sit in Meditation*

Sit in meditation.
The door of the heart opens to the inner world.
After that,
nothing is ever the same.
The knots around your life,
all the reasons for doing and not doing,
loosen and fall away.
Then, there comes the glorious choice.
Some close the door and try to go back
to an anxious way of pretending they don't know.
Others leave the door open and
walk through it to a new life,
full of wonders,
only now perceived.
Sit in meditation.
The door of the heart opens to the inner world.

■ *Desolation/Consolation*

Desolation

This house is empty
when you are away.
Even days stay dark,
sunlight on the sill
refuses to enter.

The old black lab
lays on the floor under
the window, ready to die.
Her breathing is hard
and heavy; pain fills
her body. She will not leave
without you. This
is her loyalty.

When you arrive
your footsteps say
you love her, say
you were never gone.
She leaps into your arms
and speaks your name,
at the sound of your voice
ringing in the doorway.

Consolation

When you are here
even in winter
flowers bloom.

■ *Let Your Life Open in Beauty*

To meditate is to be
like the flower at dawn
turning toward the sun.
Doing what it is naturally
inclined to do, the flower is

energized into opening.
This flower opening
is the fulfillment of life's
intention. Its beauty
is effortless.

The flower fulfills its destiny;
its beauty speaks to those
who pass by, saying:
Creator! Love! Possibility!

Each day, turn within
to the Source of life.
Be energized, be fulfilled,
let your life open in beauty.

■ The Day the Monk Slept In

When I arrived he showed me to my cabin in the woods. "Don't be disturbed if you hear the clinking of glass outside your room in the morning," he said. "It's only me." There was a shrine there. Sitting on the shrine were six large bowls filled with water, flowers, and many, maybe one hundred and eight, small cups that he filled in the morning and emptied at dusk, as an offering to the Buddha. "When in the morning? At dawn?" I asked him, my mind setting the trap to measure the depth of his commitment to prayer. Never mind all this water, I thought. What time do you get up? "Oh no, not at dawn," he smiled. "Maybe around seven or eight." "Oh," I said. I looked at him. He looked American, about thirty-five, a little overweight, friendly enough, like one of the Campbell sons, friends of my brother, we grew up with in the suburbs. Somehow on him the shaved head became a crew cut, and I found myself glancing at the running shoes peering out from under his maroon and gold robes. I liked him, but at the same time I noticed I began to worry and wonder: is there any hope for the world if the forest monks making the offerings to Buddha are now the Campbells from next door? In the morning, I woke early and waited to watch him out my window. I waited a long time. He did not come. My heart was heavy and my mind was full of judgments. In about an hour, it started to rain. It has been raining for four days now. The bowls outside my window overflow.